EASY
ENAMELING
ON METAL

EASY
ENAMELING
ON METAL

VIRGINIE FOWLER ELBERT

Photographs and illustrations by the author

Lothrop, Lee & Shepard Company
A Division of William Morrow & Company, Inc.

NEW YORK

Photographs on pages 6, 7, 8, 9, 10, and 11 courtesy of The Metropolitan Museum of Art. Page 6: Gift of J. Pierpont Morgan, 1917. Page 7: Gift of Mr. and Mrs. John Klejman, 1966. Page 8: Gift of J. Pierpont Morgan, 1917. Page 9: Gift of George Blumenthal, 1941. Page 10: The Michael Friedsam Collection, 1931. Page 11: Bequest of Catherine D. Wentworth, 1948.

Library of Congress Cataloging in Publication Data

Elbert, Virginie Fowler
   Easy enameling on metal.

   Includes index.
   SUMMARY: Directions for decorating a variety of metal objects with quick-drying, liquid enamels that do not require the use of a kiln.
   1. Enamel and enameling—Juvenile Literature.
[1. Enamel and enameling. 2. Handicraft] I. Title.
TT382.6.E38   738.4   75-16457
ISBN 0-688-41710-8
ISBN 0-688-51710-2 lib. bdg.

CONTENTS

1 / What is Enameling? / 6

2 / Tools and Metal / 14

3 / What is Cold Enamel? / 21

4 / The Finishing Touches / 29

5 / Buy It and Decorate It / 36

6 / Pieces of Metal / 53

7 / Bowls and Trays and Other Forms / 76

8 / Special Tips / 89

9 / Alphabet / 92

Sources of Supplies / 94

Index / 96

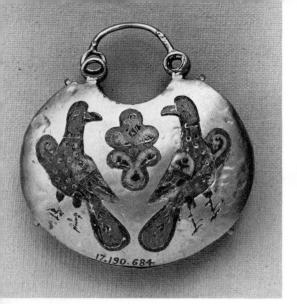

An 11-12th century Russo-Byzantine gold earring or pendant decorated with two cloisonné enamel birds.

1
WHAT IS ENAMELING?

The art of enameling—the application of a glass-like material to metal under high temperatures (1500 degrees)—is a decorative process that has been practiced since the 19th century before Christ.

Each country has had a peak time of enamel design. Many of the early designs were religious or ceremonial pieces, preserved carefully by churches or royal treasuries—or in the case of very ancient Egyptian pieces, buried in a king's tomb. There must have been a great deal of enameled jewelry worn, but pieces were lost, or went out of fashion and the precious metal was melted down for a more modern design.

An Egyptian pendant from 1900 years before Christ shows two enameled birds connected by fine gold wires and hung on a necklace of gold, green feldspar, carnelian, and lapis lazuli beads.

A Syrian ornament, made sometime in the 2nd to 3rd century when that country was a province of Rome, is in the

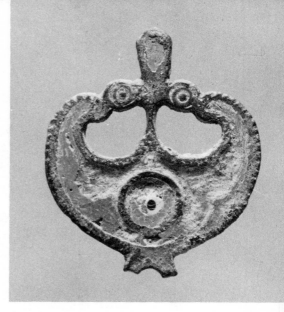

A shield-shaped ornament from the 2nd to 3rd century.

shape of a light shield, and the whole area is covered with enamel.

At the same time, the Celts in Britain decorated their bronze shields and sword handles, as well as mirrors, by pouring molten enamel into the sunken designs in the metal.

There is a piece from the 9th century in the Oxford Museum in England called The Alfred Jewel, of gold, enamel, and rock crystal, with the inscription "Alfred ordered me to be made."

Beginning with the Byzantine period in the 11th and 12th centuries, enameling seemed to develop into a skill shared in many countries, as new processes were created. The Byzantine designs were often a combination of *champlevé* and *cloisonné*. The designs were made on thin sheets of gold out of which shallow areas were scraped. The champlevé (raised field) technique involved filling these areas with enamel powders and melting the material with heat until it was

A 13th century French-Limoges casket decorated with champlevé enamel.

liquid and filled the hollows of the metal. (See page 42 for a modern use of this process).

In cloisonné (chambered partitions), the sunken areas were divided by fine gold wires and different colored enamels were added between the wires. After the enamels were melted, the surface was rubbed down with a polishing stone until enamel and wires were even. The wires were like a fine pen line, outlining a figure, or the folds of a robe, or the features of a face.

Parts of some necklaces and earrings have survived and a Byzantine one is shown on the first page of this chapter. The gold button shape has champlevé and cloisonné decorations of strutting birds.

*A pendant of gold, enamel and crystal—
The Resurrection—made in Italy in the
16th century.*

Also in the Byzantine period precious small caskets called *reliquaries* were made to hold a sacred relic—a bone of a saint, a piece of the true cross. The metal was gold, or silver, or copper gilt elaborately decorated with champlevé enamel and jewels. Sometimes the sides and the top of the boxes were covered with religious scenes, others had chiseled geometric patterns filled with enamel, as in the picture on page 8.

In China and in Japan the enamel work was mainly in cloisonné starting around the 14th century. Very elaborate metal vases and bowls were created.

In the Renaissance period beginning in the 14th century, enamels were also used to decorate elaborate pendants of gold, crystal, and jewels. These were created for wealthy families in Italy, Germany, and France. Sometimes the enamel was applied in jewel-like touches to a gold figure; other times

Orpheus attacked by the Frenzied Women. A French-Limoges enameled scene, done on copper by Suzanne Court in the late 16th century.

small enamel plaques of scenes were set into gold, surrounded by clear crystal and jewels.

As the methods of mixing and applying enamels improved, designs became more elaborate and the metal areas covered by enamel were larger. By the late 16th and 17th centuries in Limoges, France artists were creating whole scenes with enamels. These were in bright and dark colors laid on side by side, with no metal cloisonnés in between, and the enamel

A French gold snuffbox of the 18th century, decorated with blue and white enamel.

was thickly built up in many layers over a base of copper. Some designs were of mythological gods and goddesses, others were scenes from the Bible. Some of the most beautiful were done by Suzanne Court, whose husband also was an enameler.

Then came the 18th century in France with its elaborate court affairs and entertainments. Enameled snuffboxes, trinket boxes, patch boxes, and all sorts of small containers and covers were made, as small souvenirs to be given away at balls and as a memento of an occasion. The box shown here is a snuffbox of gold, decorated with panels of royal blue enamel. Details are in colored enamels on white sections. The letters are cut out of foil and held between two layers of transparent enamel, in a process called *paillons* (large spangles). See page 86.

Coming closer to our present time, the Russian jeweler Fabergé, at the end of the 19th and beginning of the 20th century, created fantastic enameled jewels, boxes, and cases for the Russian court. His Easter egg designs were incredibly beautiful and elaborate, made for an Emperor's gift to his Empress. His transparent enamels, especially a dark red, have rarely been matched.

As you work with enamels you will be able to appreciate these museum pieces even more, as you will have experienced some of the final results of these ancient artists, as well as the steps they took to make their designs.

The enamelist was a painstaking, highly-skilled craftperson. It was no easy task to make the enamel powders from a special sand mixed with the right proportions of potash and soda. Then to grind down the oxides of metals for coloring matter—cobalt for blue, copper for turquoise, uranium or antimony for yellow, tin for white, and so on. Then to melt all the ingredients together, pour out and cool the resulting cakes of glass before grinding them to the proper fineness— as fine or finer than granulated sugar. All this took skill and knowledge—and an enormous amount of time.

Each color was mixed and ground separately, as the colors could not be blended to form another color or tone.

Then the metal design to hold the enamel had to be made —in gold, or silver, or copper. Once this base was complete, the enamel was carefully and painstakingly applied, and fired in the kiln. Such projects could take a year in the making and were very expensive. Look for these rare objects in museums.

Enamels are still heated in kilns or ovens, but the powders are bought already ground, and a craftperson is still limited to three metals as a base—copper, silver, and gold.

However, we are very lucky to have available an even simpler method to achieve the effects of the old and beautiful craft, and that is what this book is all about. The exciting new liquid, cold enamels require no heat, become solid in

A gold Fabergé necklace of red enamel, topaz, and pearls, from the early 20th century.

twenty-four hours, and totally hard in a week. They are sold as liquids in both opaque and transparent colors. These liquid colors can be mixed with each other to achieve new colors, or lighter or darker tones of a single color. The material has the great advantage of being usable on *all* inexpensive metals.

In the following pages the whole emphasis is on learning the skill of enameling—an exciting and very satisfying craft. The designs in this book are of the type found in the best of craft galleries, and the quick results are beautiful, jewel-like creations of which you can be proud.

Have fun!

2
TOOLS
AND METAL

Tools for measuring and mixing enamel. Top to bottom, toothpicks, paper cup and bottle cap to hold mixed enamel, metal measuring spoons, brush, stick and glass rod for stirring, metal scriber, and riffle file.

TOOLS NEEDED

For any project one must first collect the tools and supplies, and those needed for mixing and applying liquid enamels are minimal. Many you'll find in the kitchen.

1. A set of *metal measuring spoons.*
2. Small *paper cups* to hold the enamel.
3. *Wooden* or *glass stirrers* for mixing the enamel. Wooden *tongue depressors* are good to use.
4. Soft *watercolor brushes* to apply the enamel. Their size will depend on the area to be covered.
5. *Wooden toothpicks*, and small *squeeze bottles* with metal tubes attached to their caps to make narrow lines and designs with enamel.

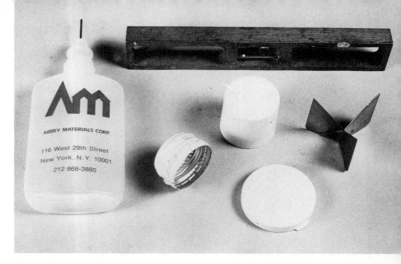

Tools used in enameling. A plastic squeeze bottle with metal tube cap, small level, bottlecaps, three-point metal stilt.

6. Small *three-point* and *four-point* stainless steel *stilts*. They are used to support small, flat metal pieces which are to be enameled on both sides. The support pressure is on the outside edge of the piece of metal, so the enameled top and bottom is suspended in mid-air. They can be obtained at craft supply stores.

7. Small 1 inch high *plastic,* or low, *metal bottlecaps* are used to support a metal shape during the enameling of the first side to prevent the enamel from running off onto the working surface.

8. Small *level.* This is an *extra* tool which can be bought in a hardware or variety store. A level will show if your working surface is even. If it slopes, adjust the surface until the level's bubble is centered in its glass tube.

9. Some of the metal forms you will buy—coasters, bowls, tiles, and other shapes, may have scratches on the surface. These are removed by rubbing the metal evenly with fine *crocus* or *carborundum cloth,* bought at a craft shop, hardware, or variety store. If this type of cloth is

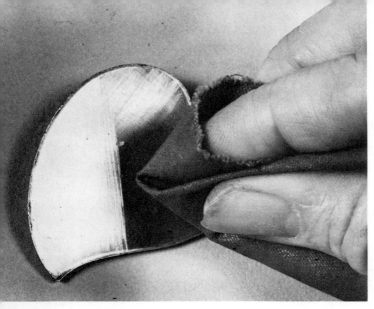

Polishing a copper shape with crocus cloth.

not available, buy the finest grain *sandpaper,* or a wetable sandpaper called *wet-and-dry.* All of these will polish metal, but will not add new scratches.

10. A double-ended *riffle file,* to make notches, and to smooth edges. These can be obtained at a craft supply store.

11. All metal to be enameled must be free of any grease, or dirt, or unseen bits of grit from the polishing material. Otherwise the enamel will not stick to the metal. Even a fingerprint is greasy, and must be cleaned off! This process is done *after* polishing. There are several materials for cleaning the metal base; *powdered kitchen cleanser, rubbing alcohol, vinegar and salt* for copper, or *clear ammonia.* And a final rinsing with *running hot water.*

12. A *metal scriber,* and *carbon paper* to trace designs on the metal surfaces (see page 28).

13. *Epoxy cement* is a strong glue which holds metal to metal, or metal to wood, and is used in attaching find-

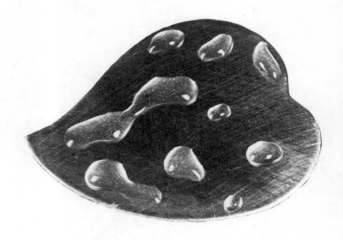

Water stays in small puddles on a greasy copper surface.

ings, jewelry designs, or metal tiles to wooden boxes. See Chapter 4 for a complete description of its use.

14. See Chapter 4 for special supplies to be used in the *finishing* of each project.

METAL BASES FOR ENAMEL

Metal is the base for all enameling. Since no heat is involved in the modern method of cold liquid enameling, metals such as *aluminum, pewter, nickel,* or any other *low melting point metal* can be used. *Brass* and *steel* are easily enameled with the liquid material, as are *copper* and *silver.* Since pewter and aluminum look like silver, and brass resembles gold, your finished projects will always have an expensive look.

There are many shapes and sizes of metal, both *flat* and *pre-formed,* which can be enameled. Specific forms will be described at the beginning of the project chapters where they are used.

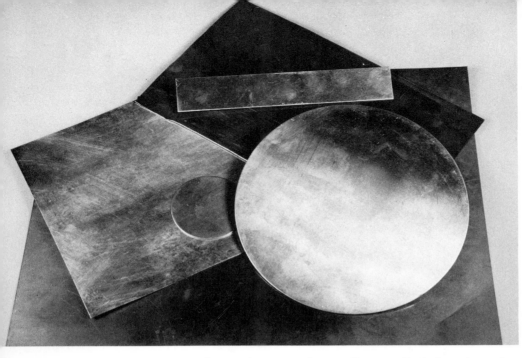

Sheets of copper, brass, silver, and circles of pewter.

Copper, silver, brass, and pewter are sold also in *sheets* of various sizes—the largest being 12 inches square. Aluminum sheets are larger. If you need a piece that is not a standard size, a craft shop might cut it for you. The thickness of metal is measured in *gauges*—the lower the gauge number, the thicker the metal. A good all-around thickness is 18 gauge.

WHERE TO BUY METAL

The metal described in the preceding section can be bought in craft shops, art stores, variety stores, hardware stores, or by mail order. Look in the yellow pages of the telephone book for craft shops near you, or look on pages 94–95 for the name of a mail order supplier in your section of the country, and send for a catalog.

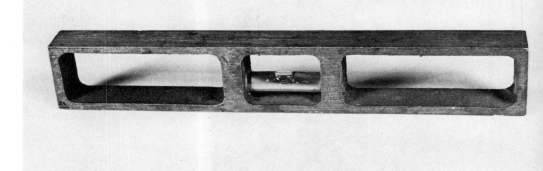

A small level, showing bubble in the middle.

PREPARING
YOUR WORKING SURFACE

Pick a place where your work can be left undisturbed for the important *first* twenty-four hours of drying. Make sure that the area is level, so that the liquid enamel will harden in an even layer on the metal base. If you find the enamel is running to one side, adjust your piece with a small wedge of paper slipped under one side. Or use a *level* to check the whole working surface (see page 15).

Cover the surface with newspaper. On top put a sheet of plastic—an opened cleaner's bag is perfect.

Gather all the materials and tools you will need, and arrange them on the plastic-covered surface.

BUT REMEMBER—in handling the metal, and especially during the final hot water rinse, your fingers must not touch the surface to be enameled. This takes careful planning! Hold the object by the edges, protect your fingers with a piece of paper towel, or wear rubber gloves.

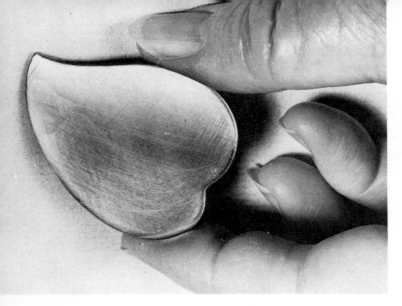

How to hold a clean piece of metal.

If water spreads evenly over the whole metal surface, then you can be sure that there are no greasy spots. But if the liquid breaks up into small puddles when you take the metal away from the running water, repeat the cleaning process.

3
WHAT IS COLD ENAMEL?

Various sizes of enamel jars and hardener containers.

Cold enamel is a two-part liquid system, consisting of a *polymer or liquid color,* plus a *hardener or curing agent.* Each product requires its own proportion of color to hardener, so be sure to check the manufacturer's instructions carefully. (See also page 89.)

There are several products available on the market. Three are suited for the projects in this book: *Spectrum 100, Boss Gloss,* and *Ceramitation.* All three brands provide both opaque and transparent enamels in 4 to 7 oz. jars, a hardener, and a thinner. Boss Gloss also has a thickener which helps to keep the enamel from flowing down the sloping sides of a bowl.

These products are used by craft people as well as by concerns manufacturing costume jewelry and can be purchased at craft shops, or ordered by mail directly from the suppliers whose names are listed on page 94.

Measuring the enamel color into a paper cup.

HOW TO MIX COLD ENAMELS

First, here are the manufacturer's suggested proportions:

Spectrum 100—two parts color to one part hardener
Boss Gloss—one part color to one part hardener
Ceramitation—two parts color to three parts hardener

Measure the color with a metal measuring spoon, pouring the liquid carefully from the bottle into the spoon. If you dip the spoon into the jar instead, be sure its surface is clean. Scrape the enamel off the spoon, and into your mixing cup, to be sure your measurements are accurate. Following the manufacturer's directions, measure out the right amount of hardener.

Now, mix both liquids together in a small paper cup. Stir them very gently with a wooden stirrer—a tongue depressor is a very good tool. Try not to get any air into the mixture, as this will cause bubbles to form. Let the mixture stand for five minutes. Any bubbles will rise to the top and pop—either with or without the help of a pinprick.

Try to judge the amount of enamel you will need, and mix just enough. For a small pendant you will be using the half-teaspoon or quarter-teaspoon measure.

Always wipe spoons clean after each use.

HOW TO CHANGE THE COLORS

The liquid, *opaque colors* can be mixed together to form other colors. They can also be blended with white or black to lighten or darken the tones. This means that you can buy a minimum of three colors—red, yellow, and blue, plus black, and white—and mix them to form many colors and shades.

The *transparent colors* are mixed in the same way. A little transparent color added to clear enamel will make a paler, transparent color. A very little white swirled into a transparent color (but not fully mixed) will result in a cloudy-clear opal look.

Always mix the colors together *first,* then measure the result before adding the hardener, so you are sure to add the right amount of hardener.

If the mixed enamel is too thick, *a thinner* can be added. If you do this, remember to measure out the right proportion of hardener for this additional liquid.

HOW TO APPLY
THE MIXED ENAMEL

Once the enamel has been well mixed, and allowed to rest

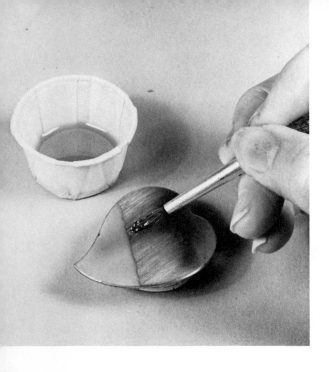

Applying mixed enamel to a copper leaf form.

for five minutes, apply it in a thin coat to the metal surface with a soft, pointed brush.

When this is the first layer of a solid color, or a colored base coat under a design, let the surface dry for six to eight hours until it is *tacky*. If your piece is to be finished in just a solid color, check to see if the surface needs a second coat. If so, add it now, and let the object stay undisturbed on a level area for twenty-four hours before moving the piece.

Some enamels will cover the metal evenly with one coat. Other enamel finishes look far better with two, or even three coats. All the variations of room temperature, the thickness of the coat, the evenness of application, the type of enamel (opaque or transparent), the color of the metal, play a part in the final enamel surface.

In the project descriptions, directions will only be given to *"cover the metal with enamel,"* but you will have to decide how many coats to put on the metal so that the finished product looks best.

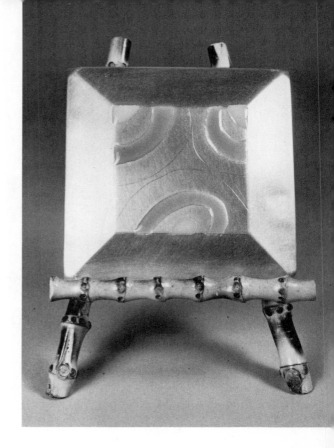

Two colors applied to a design. When dry, the other two enamel colors will be added.

When a design of a second color is being added and the base color is even enough, the design can be painted on after that first layer has dried for eight hours. Then let everything dry for twenty-four hours.

For a striped design in several colors, or a pattern of different colors, you do not need a solid base coat. Put on the first color, and let it dry for about an hour. Now add the next color beside it. Since the first color has dried a bit, the two liquids should not run into each other. Repeat for each color. If a second coat is needed, let the whole design dry for eight hours, and then add fresh enamel. Dry for twenty-four hours.

As you can tell from this description, freshly-applied wet

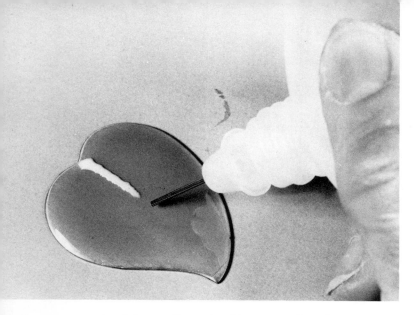

Applying a line of white enamel with a squeeze bottle.

colors will blend together. But you may want this to happen, so experiment with the effect.

Another method is to cover the metal with a base coat of clear enamel. After this has dried for eight hours, add area designs but leave a narrow line of clear enamel between each color. This means you can put all the colors on at once without waiting an hour for each one to dry. But this method needs a steady hand! Or make the line between colors a little wider, as a feature of your design. The clear enamel keeps the exposed areas of copper or brass from tarnishing.

Enamel can be applied in lines or swirled designs from a squeeze bottle. It can be dropped as pools of color from a toothpick or brush. Opaque enamels can be applied to contrast with transparent enamels. Transparent enamels can be used to decorate flat, opaque enamel surfaces, or as a coating over opaque decorations.

Lumps of transparent and opaque enamel and assorted enamel threads, with small tweezer.

SPECIAL EFFECTS

Threads and lumps of enamel are made commercially from regular glass enamel. Buy them in craft shops in small jars or boxes, either transparent or opaque or a mixture of both.

These are added to the final surface of enamel while it is still tacky. The pieces are put in position with a tweezer, and very gently pressed into the enamel. Once the surface has dried, a clear coat of enamel can be added over the whole surface if the threads seem to be loose.

Aluminum or gold colored foil is cut into small shapes, then laid on top of an almost dry first layer of transparent enamel. The whole surface is covered by a second coat of transparent enamel, embedding the shimmering foil in color.

DRYING THE ENAMEL

After the *first* twenty-four hours of hardening, the enamel will be stiff, and the object can be moved. Now is the time to enamel the other side of a flat piece of metal, supporting it on a 3-point stilt (see page 15). This will hold the enameled piece by the edges so that the decorated surface is suspended in mid-air. Let the second side dry for twenty-four hours after its final coat of enamel.

After twenty-four hours of drying, let the piece stay in one spot undisturbed and with no pressure on the surface *for one week*. Resist touching the enamel, so that there will be no chance of a cloudy, marred finish.

TRANSFERRING DESIGNS TO METAL

This is a basic process, and applies to almost all the designs in this book. (See also pages 90–91.)

Draw a pencil outline of your metal shape to size on a piece of white paper. Add the design, exactly as you want it to appear on the metal. Next, put a piece of *carbon paper* over the polished metal, carbon side down. On top of this, place your paper pattern in position over the metal, and with a sharp pencil or ball-point pen trace the outlines of the design.

Remove the pattern and carbon paper from the metal, and follow the carbon line with the *scriber*. You will have a permanent line scratched into the metal. This line can be seen through transparent enamel, and, if you are using opaque enamel, you can fill in the outline with colors.

Clean off the carbon lines with rubbing alcohol, and finish cleaning the metal, following directions on page 16.

4
THE
FINISHING
TOUCHES

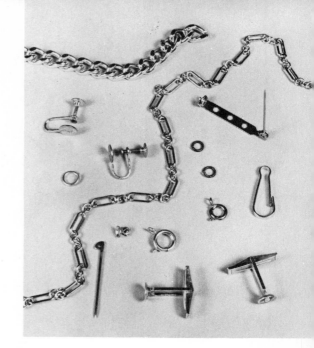

Jewelry findings—chains, earring backs, bar pin back, jump rings, catch and pin stem, spring catches, spring hook, and cuff link backs.

Many of the projects in the following chapters need finishing touches for wearing or displaying them, so here are the instructions for those final details.

For all the jewelry projects you should buy what are called *findings*. These are *pin backs, earring backs, cuff link backs,* small rings and loops called *jump rings,* and ring *safety catches.*

You will also need *chains* for necklaces and bracelets, and thin *bead-stringing wire.*

Findings and chains are bought at craft supply shops or by mail order, and some can be bought in variety stores.

Pin backs are of two types. One is a flat bar with holes along its length, with the pin and catch at opposite ends. This is the easiest type to apply and has the strongest hold.

*Pin back held in place with epoxy
cement.*

The other is in two parts—the catch, and the pin on a riveted hinge. These two pieces can be put on as close or as far apart as the length of the pin. Buy the type with small cups on the bottom to hold epoxy.

To apply a pin back to an enameled metal form, mix an epoxy cement according to directions on the two tubes. Spread a thick strip of cement where you want to put the pin back. Always attach it above the center line of a form, so the finished brooch will not fall forward when it is worn.

Let the epoxy thicken for a few minutes, then press the pin back bar into the liquid. The cement should ooze up through the holes and flow over their edges for a better grip. *But* be sure that the pin can still swing freely on its rivet. Let dry for 24 hours.

If the back of the form will be covered with cold, liquid enamel you can push the pin back into this material before it is dry. Then, when you add a second coat of enamel, cover the metal bar, too.

Cuff links and *earring backs* are attached to enameled forms with epoxy cement in the same manner as pin backs.

Spools of copper and brass wire with wire cutter and chain nose pliers.

Pendants and charms are attached to chains or neck wires by *jump rings*, which are made from round or flat wire in either oval or round shapes. They are made of copper, silver, gold-filled, or a base metal in several sizes, and are sold singly or in packets in craft shops, or by mail order.

The joining edges of the rings are closed. To open them enough to attach either metal forms or two rings together, you will need a pair of *chain nose pliers*, which are pliers with long pointed tips. You also can use household pliers. After opening, slip one side of the ring through the hole in your metal piece, then squeeze the two ends together again with the pliers.

To buy the right length of *chain* for a necklace or bracelet, use a piece of string to measure your neck or wrist. For both short chain necklaces and bracelets you will have to attach a jump ring and a ring catch at one end, and a jump ring at the other. You can also buy finished chain necklaces and bracelets in variety stores.

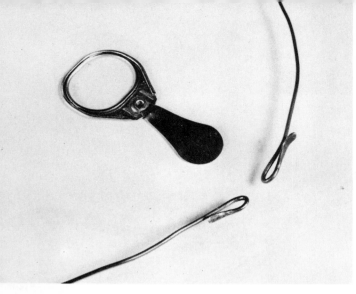

The tab from a soft drink can, and hooks formed at the ends of a neckwire.

For wire neck wires or hanging hooks or loops for pendants, buy *brass* or *copper wire* on wooden spools which are sold in craft shops and hardware stores. Choose the thickness that you will need. Variety stores also sell shorter lengths of copper wire in small coils in the electrical supply department. A recycling wire is *bailing wire* which is wrapped around bundles of newspapers when they are delivered to the newsstand or store. Ask for a piece—it's free!

In making a *neckwire*, the first step is to measure the base of your neck with string. Cut *copper, brass,* or newspaper *bailing wire* with a *clipper,* 1⅛ inches longer than the string. Bend the wire around a *coffee* or *paint* can, to form it into a circle. To make the catch, pound ¼ inch of one end with a *hammer* until flat and oval, then round the end with a file. Now bend ⅝ inches of this end with the *pliers,* forming a hook. Bring the end all the way back until it touches the rest of the wire. Now slip the jump ring and pendant over the other end. Form the second hook, and your necklace is finished.

Small enameled tiles glued to the top of a wooden box.

To hang pendants without a top hole, or wall plaques, loops of flat wire can be attached to the back with *epoxy cement* (see page 30). For wall plaques, a very handy and inexpensive loop—no cost at all—is the tab one pulls off the top of a soft drink can. It has a round loop, and a flat piece of metal. Glue this flat piece of metal to the back of a large square or round of enameled metal. Wipe the edges clean, and put a weight over the metal tab for 24 hours, to be sure of a tight fit.

Enamel pictures are fitted to small *wooden frames* bought at art or variety stores. Frame these without glass. For eye-catching decorations, hang on the wall, or display on small *bamboo easels* which are sold in some novelty and gift shops.

To decorate unfinished *wooden boxes* with enameled plaques or mosaics, decide first on the finish of the box. You may want to use a wood stain covered with *shellac, varnish,* or *wax.* Or *enamel paint* over a first coat of *shellac,* for a colorful glossy finish. A lot depends on your own taste, and the

Sculptured metal tiles applied to box lid, using oblongs of wood.

color scheme of the room the box is to be in. Also the cold enamel decorations and colors of the small metal squares, and the box finish should be an entire design. The same methods of attachment will be used around *mirror frames, covering a wooden tray,* or small *table top.*

You have two choices of "stickums." *Epoxy cement* is a good all-around permanent glue (see page 16.) Follow the manufacturer's directions, but in general, equal quantities of liquid from the two tubes are mixed together on a smooth surface (a piece of *plastic food wrap* or *aluminum foil* will do). Cover each facing surface with the mixture, and press together. You may have to put a coat of epoxy on a porous wood surface and let it dry for two hours. Then add a second coat, covering the whole area which will contain the enameled design. Cover the back of the metal squares or plaque. After putting the metal in position, place a weight over it, and let dry for 24 hours.

The other material is an *asphalt mastic,* used to attach

vinyl tiles to a floor, or cork to a wall. This is useful for large flat squares of metal. Be sure, though, that the pieces of metal fit tightly against each other, so that the *mastic* does not ooze up between them. Follow the directions on the can for applying the material.

Attaching sculptured metal tiles (see page 64) to a box top or mirror frame, is a separate technique. Cut small, oblong pieces of *wood* 1¼ x 1½ inches, and as deep as the enameled metal tile. Glue each piece to the top surface of the wooden box, or the mirror frame, in the center of the area where each tile belongs—using epoxy cement. When solidly dry (overnight), add epoxy to the top of each block, and match with epoxy on the underside of each tile. Also put a narrow line of epoxy on the box top where the edges of the tiles will rest. Now, put the tiles in position, and add a weight on top—two or three heavy books—and let dry for 24 hours. Then admire your strikingly colorful box.

As you start to make a few of the projects in this book, you will suddenly find that you have many beautiful objects—to wear, to use, and to give away as presents. And you will probably end up making all of them! So, happy enameling, as you turn to the design pages which follow.

5
BUY IT
AND
DECORATE IT

Metal shapes. A light-switch plate, a decorative brass circle.

Now, to start the cold enamel projects let's decorate some manufactured metal products.

Look around your local hardware and variety stores or gift shops for small metal objects to decorate. You will see *coat hooks, metal doorknobs, drawer pulls, decorative furniture hardware,* and *light-switch plates.* Metal *gallery wire* is sold by the foot in hardware stores, and comes in a number of widths and pierced designs—perfect for bracelets. *Key rings*

A *large drawer pull or door knocker (right), an oblong drawer pull (below).*

are sold with metal charms or initials attached. Look at the cosmetic counters for *compacts,* or *pillboxes.* The jewelry counters have *plain metal designs* which can be enameled. Find larger *metal boxes,* or *small metal trays* or *coasters.* Serving *knives, forks,* or *spoons* which have metal handles can be another project.

Once you start looking for metal objects, the list grows and grows. And the designs shown in this book are only the beginning—you will think of many more.

Check up on the *doorknobs,* or *draw pulls* around the house, as possibilities for enameling. *But remember* that enamel takes several days to dry—so don't enamel a well-used doorknob! You might end up with a well-enameled hand!

In this chapter, a number of different designs are shown for each object. Your additions of enamel will change the product into a true original. So, follow the basic directions in Chapter Three, and have fun with the designs that follow.

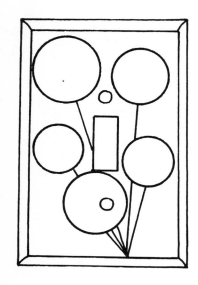

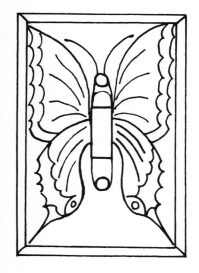

LIGHT-SWITCH COVER OR PLATE

Let's start with a plain rectangle of metal—a light-switch cover, or plate. Finished in silver, gold, or bronze color, it makes an excellent basic shape for many designs.

First, put the switch plate on a piece of white paper, right side up. Trace around the edges with a pencil. Make several tracings and use them for designing different patterns.

The simplest project is to cover the switch plate with a solid color which matches or contrasts with the walls of the room. Put on one thin coat of enamel, let it dry, then apply another thin coat.

Now try a design for fun. This project could be for a bedroom. Enamel the top half of a switch plate in green, let it dry, and then enamel the bottom half in red. Green for light on, red for light off.

Try a butterfly, a black-eyed Susan, two fishes, a green vine, balloons, or a maze. Be sure and let the enamel dry between applications of colors.

COASTERS

Metal coasters can be decorated and used as is, or they can be used as small wall plaques. Cement a soft-drink can tab on the back as a hanger.

Cover the metal completely with a transparent or opaque color. Put on the first coat, let dry, then add the second thin coat.

Top a coat of pale yellow enamel with 5 or 6 triangular segments in orange enamel—to give the effect of an orange slice. Or add a circular design to turn the coaster into a target or maze.

Scratch a design (perhaps a sailboat) into the metal with a scriber. Cover the whole surface with transparent color— and the design will show through.

Or scratch an initial into the metal with a scriber. Cover all the metal with transparent blue enamel. When it is dry, fill in the outline of the initial with a bright transparent or opaque enamel.

GALLERY WIRE BRACELET

Gallery wire, a metal edging, is thin and flat, and is usually gold in color. Ranging in width from ½ to 1 inch, or sometimes wider, it is pierced in various designs.

Measure your arm with a piece of string. Buy enough gallery wire to make a bracelet.

Turn the wire into an open-ended bracelet, with the ends ½ to ¾ inches apart. The bracelet should be large enough to slip over your hand without stretching, which might crack the enamel.

Bend the wire around a rolling pin. Take it off and carefully form it into an oval to fit your wrist. Slightly round the points of each end with a file, so they will not scratch your arm. Polish and clean the metal.

Now choose your colors, and enamel the bracelet in a solid color, or accent the design in several colors.

Examples of brass gallery wire.

FINGER RINGS AND PENDANTS

Gallery wire is often used for commercial rings or scarf holders. Look at the jewelry counters of your local variety stores for examples. You might leave the center of the ring plain, and enamel the top and bottom strips the same color, or contrasting colors.

Back again to the hardware store for heavy, round, decorative pieces of metal. These 1¼ inch wide circles have designs embossed on them. With a loop of wire on the back, you have a pendant.

Add colored enamels to the different parts of the pattern. Using transparent enamels, make the leaves green, the background orange, and the center red or yellow.

COAT HOOKS

Another interesting and useful design is a decorative coat hook.

The seahorse shown in the illustration is a perfect subject for transparent turquoise blue enamel. A thin coat of color will sink into the indentations, creating a two-tone effect. Or you can just fill in the hollows, leaving the metal ridges slightly exposed—areas of enamel separated by metal.

Or fill the hollows with different colors.

When you buy the hook, look at other metal holders which might be used for enameling—towel rings or metal drinking glass holders, for instance.

DECORATIVE
METAL HARDWARE

Decorative animal and flower designs
are fun to work on. The rooster is just
one example. Decorate the gold-colored
metal with green, rust, and yellow.
When the enamel is hard, cement on
a pin back, and you will have an elegant
pin to wear.

Some furniture decorations lend
themselves nicely to enameling; brass
corners, plaques for Chinese chests,
flowers in baskets, door knockers, and
many geometric designs.

DRAWER PULLS
OR HANDLES

These are sold in several shapes; round knobs, circular, concave or convex, oval, square, rectangular, long and narrow.

When planning your design, the first decision is a color to match or contrast the colors in the room. You can decorate the handles in solid color enamel, or add a design to them. The mood can be serious or fun, depending on the room and the style of furniture.

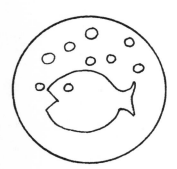

For the kitchen, you might add small drawings of kitchen utensils, or vegetables. For a game room, how about tennis racquets, golf clubs, or sailboats. In other rooms you might use designs to match the upholstery, the walls, or the curtains.

In your own room, decorate oval-shaped handles as eyes to watch over your belongings.

For other suggestions, study the drawings all around the edges of these two pages.

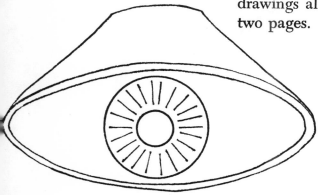

DOORKNOBS

Doorknobs are manufactured in almost as many shapes as drawer pulls. But they are larger in size so you can develop more complicated designs for them.

The designs which are shown on these two pages can be adapted for knobs or pulls. The enameling process is the same—and the choice of colors is yours.

KEY CHAIN CHARMS

If you see a key chain with an interesting metal charm, buy it and decorate it. Here are two examples: one is a turtle with a movable head and legs; the other is a block initial.

The turtle can be enameled in transparent green and brown, brown around the edges and green in the center. If you want to, put an opaque white initial in the center section. Or use unusual colors, like orange and blue.

The initial charm is enameled in any transparent or opaque color. It could be striped in opaque red and white or any other combination of colors.

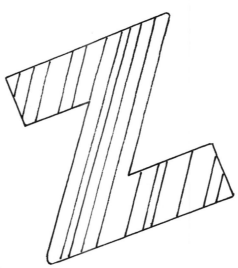

METAL BOXES

Small or medium-size metal boxes offer many possibilities for design. Some are plain, others have etched designs, and still others have raised decorations.

This French-style oval jewel box, with its dainty legs, can be enameled in several different ways, with many color combinations.

For instance, the background could be a dark transparent blue, and the scrolls white. A transparent rust-red background with emerald green scrolls is another option. Reverse the blue-and-white theme with an opaque white background and blue scrolls at the ends and in the middle. Enamel the scrolls in-between turquoise blue, and the center dark blue with tiny gold dots.

Try experimenting with crayons on white paper for other attractive color combinations.

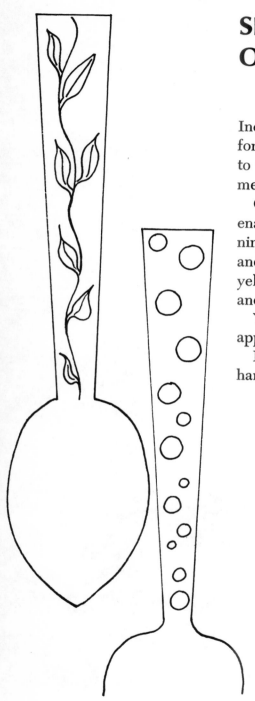

SERVING SPOON OR FORK HANDLE

Inexpensive serving spoons and forks for salads and vegetables are interesting to work with. Look for ones with plain metal handles.

Cover the handle with a solid white enamel. When it has dried, add a running leaf design, brown for the stem, and green for the leaves. Or do a solid yellow handle with polka dots in red and orange.

You can even add a design without applying a solid background.

It is best to wash these utensils by hand, so they will not be scratched.

CARPET TACK DESIGN

Copper or other metal tacks are the smallest pieces of metal you will enamel, and you can make wonderful designs with them.

Draw a pattern on a block of wood with chalk. Try a fish design. Hammer the tacks part way into the wood to outline the fish. The heads should be well above the surface of the block. Fill in some of the areas, but leave others vacant.

When you have cleaned off the metal, enamel the tops of the tacks. Try various shades of blues and greens. Let dry for a week.

Use as a paperweight, or attach a rope to the sides of the wood with nails, and hang on the wall.

RECYCLED CANS

This coaster project starts with shallow, round cans—meat spread, cat food, tuna fish, to name a few. Remove the paper labels, and wash the cans until they are clean.

Enamel the *sides*, both inside and out, with opaque enamel mixed with thickener. Put on a very thin coat, let dry, then add a second coat. Once the sides are dry, add the enamel design to the bottom—using one of the coaster or doorknob designs on pages 39, 44, and 45.

Or make a design around the outside, then cover the whole inside with a single color opaque enamel. Use the finished cans to hold paper clips or rubber bands on your desk.

TAB BRACELET
OR NECKLACE

Ask all your friends to save the tabs
from their soft drink cans. You will need
between 8 or 10 tabs for a bracelet, 24
for a short necklace, and 36 for a long
necklace.

Carefully bend one tab over the metal
ring of another tab. Bring it all the way
back until it starts through its own ring.
Repeat with all the tabs, until they are
linked into a chain.

Stretch the chain flat on your working surface. Cover the exposed tabs with
either transparent or opaque enamel,
choosing a favorite color. Do not enamel
the first tab, as this will be your catch.
You may have to tighten and loosen
it a little bit each time you wear the
bracelet or necklace and this movement
might scratch the enamel surface.

If you make a long necklace to slip
over your head, you can enamel all the
tabs.

Let dry well until hard, then wear
happily.

HANG UP
THE WASHERS

Buy three sizes of bright-finished, thin metal washers. Get six of each size— ⅞ inch, ¾ inch, and 9/16 inch.

Make a notch with a file on the outside edge of each washer, and a matching one on the inside circle. Tightly wrap two or three rows of fine wire around the washers, connecting the notches. Twist together about two inches of the two ends of wire, cut off, and form a ⅜ inch hook.

Enamel the washers with a coat of opaque enamel of your choice. Cover the wrapped wire areas, too. When dry, add various width stripes of a second color. These stripes also can be several colors, either transparent, or opaque, or a mixture of both.

When the washers are hard and dry, turn over and cover the back with solid color enamel. When dry, hang the circles, by the twisted wire, on a chain necklace.

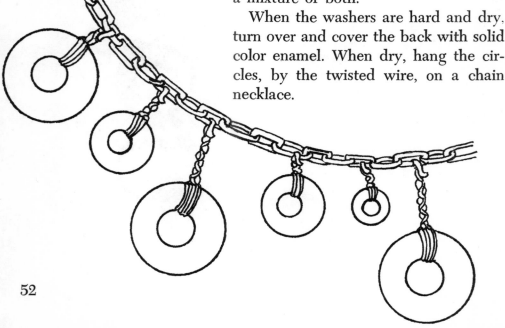

6
PIECES
OF METAL

Geometric copper shapes.

You can buy small *aluminum, copper,* and *silver* shapes in a number of sizes at art or craft stores, the hobby section of a department store, or by mail order from a craft supply company. The copper, and sometimes the silver forms are made in *squares, circles, ovals, triangles, rectangles, diamonds,* as well as *four-leaf clovers, hearts, seahorses, butterflies, free-form,* and many other shapes. Many of these have a small hole at the top so they can be hung on a chain or neck wire as pendants or charms.

One-inch squares of copper can be set as mosaics or miniature tiles on the top of a *wooden* or *metal box,* which is purchased in art and craft shops.

Larger squares, flat or raised, of copper, pewter, aluminum,

Decorative copper shapes.

or brass are used as the base for geometric designs, or pictorial scenes which are framed and set on a miniature bamboo easel. Try covering a wooden tray with the tiles, or framing a mirror with bright designs.

In this chapter you'll find several different designs for each project. As you work along, be sure that:

1. You follow the instructions in Chapter 2 for polishing and cleaning the metal base—and in Chapter 3 for mixing and applying cold enamel.
2. Check the directions in Chapter 3 for transferring your design to metal.
3. When using enamel threads for designs (pages 70–71) make a full size "mock-up" of your pattern on a piece of white paper, laying the threads in position. Then when you transfer them with the tweezer to the tacky enamel surface, there will be no mistakes.

ALL SORTS OF "MOUNTINGS"

Mounting is a jeweler's name for a form on which cut and polished stones can be *mounted* (or added) with epoxy cement. Look in a craft store or a jewelry-craft catalog for earring, pin, cuff link, tie clasp, tie tack, bracelet, or pendant forms which are made especially for cemented-on stones.

These same mountings can be used as a background for enamel. In place of a stone, the flat area up to the rim of metal can be filled with two or three coats of transparent or opaque colored enamel. Some of the metal surfaces are patterned, and these make interesting designs under transparent enamels.

Brooch pin mountings in peacock, owl, clown, spray of flowers, or Christmas tree designs are covered with small depressions made to hold tiny stones. Instead, drop transparent enamel into each hole, and let dry. The pin will sparkle with enamel "jewels."

This is a fun project, and very simple to do.

A METAL BRACELET

Buy a copper bracelet kit made especcially for enameling. Or a metal bracelet made to hold cemented-on stones. The flat metal links, ovals, squares, and heart shapes can be easily enameled. Their white or yellow-gold color, and embossed surfaces are just right for transparent enamels.

Now use your imagination for wild color combinations in either transparent or opaque enamels or both together. Here are some possibilities: two colors alternating; a different color for each link; geometric designs of two or more colors; a name or a nickname spelled out—it's all yours.

Cover both sides of the metal, following the directions in Chapter Three. Be sure to keep the holes free of enamel. Twirl a round toothpick in each hole while the enamel is still wet.

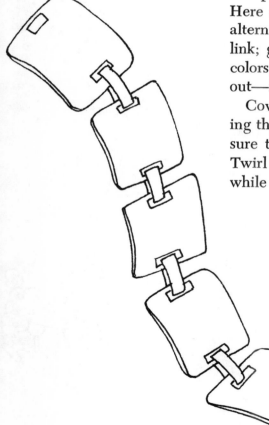

A VALENTINE BRACELET

This is a loving project, a present for a good friend—and very easy to make.

Buy four copper heart shapes, 1⅛ inches wide. These will have a loop at the top so that they can be hung by a jump ring to a chain bracelet.

Now put a thin coat of transparent red enamel over each heart. Let dry, and add a second coat if needed. Dry again, this time for 24 hours. Turn the hearts over, and enamel the other side. See pages 27-28.

Now add a tiny pink heart of opaque enamel in the middle of each charm. Or add a white enameled letter on each heart, so that the four together spell L O V E.

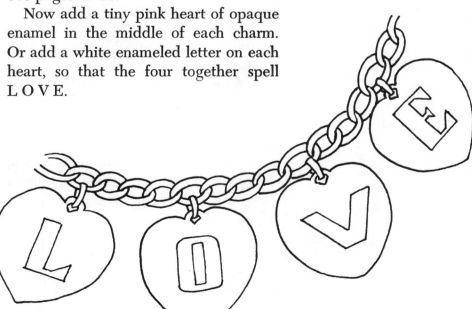

A TUBE NECKLACE

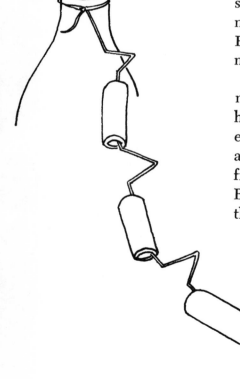

This necklace is made from ⅝ inch lengths of brass tubing, called *sleeves*, which can be bought in fishing tackle departments, twelve to a box. Added to these are gold-tone metal beads, either pierced or plain, which can be bought in craft shops, or at department or variety stores. You will also need a fine chain to string them on.

Measure around the base of your neck with a piece of string. A good length is just below your collarbone. Stretch the string flat on a table top, and plan how many tubes and beads you will need. For 18 inches, you will need approximately 20 sleeves, and 20 ¼-inch beads.

During enameling, the tubes should not touch the working surface. And here's how the trick is done. Wrap one end of a 30-inch length of fine wire around the top of a soda bottle. Slip the free end of the wire through a tube. Before adding the next tube, squeeze the wire into an upward pointing triangle, which will separate the two tubes. Slip the second tube on the wire, make the triangle, slip on the next tube —until all tubes are strung on the wire. Now wrap the end of the wire around a second soda bottle, and your tightrope trick is done. Use this method whenever you have to enamel round beads, or tubes.

Enamel ⅓ of each tube with transparent or opaque red. Dry a bit, then enamel the next section in green, and let dry. Enamel the last section in orange. Or try dark pink opaque, medium pink, light pink, and green.

When completely dry, string the tubes on a fine chain, alternating with the metal beads. Add a catch and ring at opposite ends.

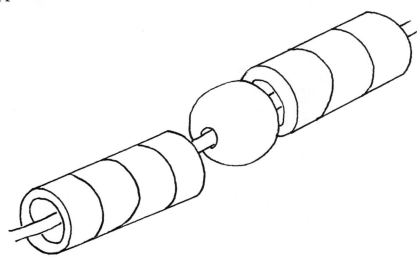

A TEARDROP
PENDANT

A 2-inch long, egg-shaped copper form is the basis for this pendant, which can be hung in the center of the tube necklace.

Follow the design in the margin, adding the enamels—red, green, and orange. Start at the outer edge with a border of light orange with red rectangles. Next a bright green, then dark orange, now a white in the center, with bright green lines finishing things off. Let each area dry before adding the next color.

You can also change the colors to match the enamels you have chosen for the brass tubes of the necklace. After the piece has dried, turn it over, and cover the back with clear, transparent enamel. This will prevent the copper from tarnishing.

When the back is thoroughly dry, hang the pendant from a necklace or chain with oval jump rings.

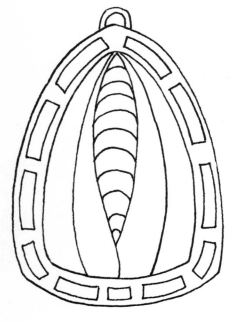

A SUN GOD PENDANT

Buy a round copper disk, 2 inches wide. Try to find one with a loop at the top. If you can't, add a wire loop, using epoxy cement. Scratch in the design with a scriber, and wipe clean again.

Cover the front of the pendant with a thin coat of colorless, transparent enamel. Dry for at least eight hours.

Now paint the design, following the outlines you have marked into the metal. The outside border of each flame is opaque white, the next area a light yellow, the center area orange. The round sun face is also orange. Use a toothpick to draw in the features in red.

Put each color on separately, and allow drying times so that they will not run into each other. The center circle will have to dry the longest so you can put the eyes, nose, and mouth over the orange enamel.

When dry, turn over the disk, support it on a three point stilt, (see page 15), and put a coat of clear enamel on the back. Let the pendant dry for a week before adding the jump ring.

SMALL COPPER TILES

The fascinating part of making designs with small copper squares, and using several of them together, is finding the many new patterns which develop. See what happens when you put four tiles together in a square, or six tiles in a rectangular shape. Or place them as diamond shapes around a circle to form a kaleidoscope pattern.

Around the edges of this page and the next are several ideas which should make you think of many more.

Cut out a number of one inch squares of paper. Make the same design on several of them. Move the squares

around to form new designs. Finally, transfer a favorite one to squares of copper. Enamel with transparent or opaque enamels, or a combination of both.

These mosaics can be used to cover a part or the whole of a wooden box top, set into small trays, or used as borders around small mirrors or pictures.

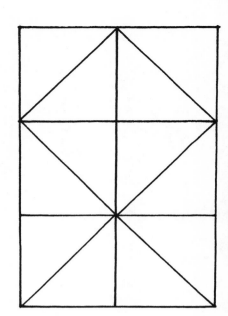

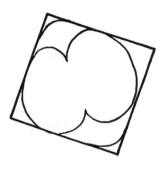

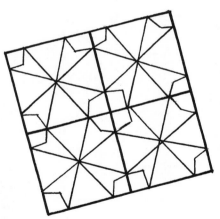

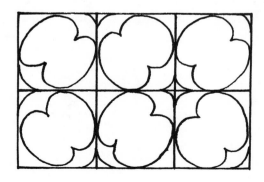

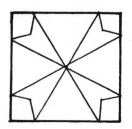

SCULPTURED TILES

Center design, starting from edge—pink, magenta red, light green, lavender. Sides are plain aluminum.

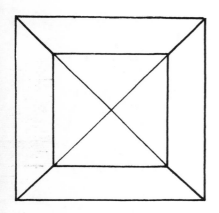

Center design, top and bottom triangles—light red, left and right triangles—light green. Top and left side— light yellow, bottom and right side—light orange.

These are aluminum forms 3¾ inches square.

The tiles can be used as single units and hung on the wall as pictures, or set as a single tile on the top of a box. They can also be used in groups to cover a large box top, or a wall, or cabinet area. In this case the designs should be arranged so that they will form a unified pattern.

Make a sketch of the design you want to use, and plan your colors with crayons. The slanting border can be all one color, or two sides one color, the other sides a second color. The center a contrasting solid color.

Other suggestions include; patterned edges and solid center, solid color edges with a center pattern, or both edges and center patterned.

Adapt this form to designs for either the convex, or concave side—and see how clever you can be. The concave side forms a frame and miniature picture area—all in one.

These are suggested colors. You can use either opaque or transparent colors, or use both on the same design. Try out other combinations with colored pencils on white paper.

Alternating blue and green lines against plain aluminum metal sides. Center is covered with pale transparent blue, topped with opaque orange fishes.

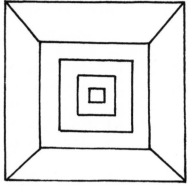

Solid blue or purple sides. Outside center border—magenta red, then yellow-green, next deep pink, and finally dark blue.

Outside triangles on sides are a bright blue. Inside triangles a deep yellow. Outside center border—bright blue, then deep yellow, magenta red, light yellow, and orange.

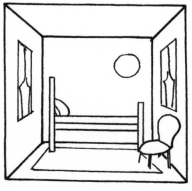

Walls and floor pale blue. Rug orange. Ceiling and windows turquoise blue. Bed, mirror, and chair-dark blue.

A NAMEPLATE

Two types of nameplates can be made from rectangular pieces of aluminum. Hobby shops sell 22 gauge strips, 1 x 6 inches. The metal is stiff enough to hold its shape, yet thin enough so that a hole can be made in each corner without using a drill.

To do this, use a small nail or brad. Place the metal on a block of wood. Hammer the nail right through the metal, from front to back. Put a hole in each corner if the nameplate is to be attached to a door. If it is to be hung by a cord or chain, then it needs only a hole at each top corner. Smooth the edges of the holes with a file.

Next, enlarge or reduce by squares the letters you need, using the alphabet on page 92. Place these in position on a piece of paper the exact size of the metal. Trace them onto the metal, using carbon paper. Take a ruler, and follow the carbon lines with the scriber. Wash off the carbon with rubbing alcohol.

Cover the metal with a transparent color enamel of your choice. The outlines of the letters drawn on the metal will show through the transparent en-

amel. When the enamel is hard, fill in the letters with a contrasting opaque enamel, keeping within the outlines of the letters.

A FREE-STANDING NAMEPLATE

For this project you will need a wider piece of metal which will be folded down the middle at a right angle.

Draw a line lengthwise across the middle of the piece of metal with the scriber, using the edge of a ruler. Put the metal on a table with the folding line even with the edge. Brace the table side of the metal with one hand, and slowly bend down the other half against the edge of the table.

Add the lettering on the front half of the metal with the scriber, as described on the opposite page.

Now proceed with the enameling, keeping the metal flat. Place the plate on a block of wood, with the working surface facing up, and the back against the side. Follow the enameling directions on the opposite page.

A PICTURE TILE

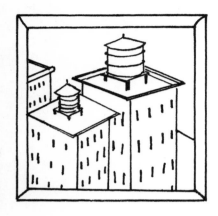

On a 4 x 4 inch square of metal—aluminum, brass, copper, or pewter—"paint" an enamel picture.

Using the same techniques of applying enamel as you used for small tiles or coasters, make a small scene. Your own room or house, a view from your window, a favorite vacation place, a pet, a plant, a pair of boots, an historical monument—these are only a few suggestions. Your picture can end at the metal edge, or you can enamel a frame all around the edge.

After the picture has dried for a week, frame it, or put it on display on a bamboo easel.

Or, make a scene that covers four or six or more tiles, and use these to decorate a tray or small table top.

BUTTERFLY PIN

A copper butterfly shape 1½ x 1 inches is the basis of an enameled pin.

Cover the two wings with medium blue opaque enamel. When dry, paint the body with brown opaque enamel. Now outline the wings with ⅛ inch of brown. Add an orange spot on each lower and upper wing, or enamel lumps.

When the enamels are thoroughly dry, turn over the pin. Cover the back with clear enamel—except for the pin back area. When dry and hard, glue on the pin back.

Try other color combinations and designs. Look in the encyclopedia for color photographs of butterflies and moths, or look in a nature study guide for other butterfly designs to copy. You can also use transparent enamels, with accent spots of opaque enamel.

A PENDANT OF SUNBURST THREADS

Enamel threads of assorted colors—all opaque or all transparent—are sold in small boxes. Sometimes one can buy a mixture of the two types.

Start this project by buying an oval copper pendant, 2 inches long. Cover the front with transparent bright yellow enamel. When the enamel has reached the tacky stage, use a tweezer to arrange the threads in a sunburst pattern. Work slowly, as the threads cannot be moved once they have touched the enamel.

When thoroughly dry, turn over and cover the back with yellow enamel. When dry, slip a jump ring through the top hole and hang the pendant on a chain.

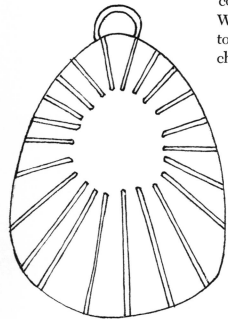

STICK FIGURES

Start with an oblong piece of aluminum 1 x 6 inches. Punch a small hole in each corner (see page 66 for directions).

Cover the metal with a coat of transparent enamel in a light color. When the enamel has reached the tacky stage, arrange your pattern of enamel thread figures in a line. Use tweezers to put the threads on the enamel surface. Use lumps of enamel for the heads, or add small drops of contrasting enamel *after* the background enamel has dried. Attach to the middle of a box with small nails.

Add single stick figures to 1 inch squares of metal. Hang them on a chain with jump rings as a necklace or bracelet.

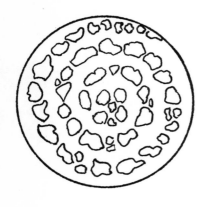

LUMPY SNAIL SHELLS

Start with a 2 inch round of copper or aluminum, which will be used for either a pendant or a pin.

Cover the metal with opaque enamel in a light color. When the enamel has dried to the tacky stage, place transparent enamel lumps in a spiral pattern with the tweezers. Start at the outer edge, and circle inward to the center, pressing down each lump for a good contact with the enamel.

When the enamel is very hard and dry, turn the circle over and brace it on a metal stilt. If you are planning to wear the snail as a pendant, cover the back with a coat of the same opaque enamel as you used on the front. Press a loop of wire into the enamel when it begins to thicken. Dry and add a second coat to be sure that the wire is well covered by the enamel.

You can use the same technique when adding a pin back (see page 30).

This design can be used on small circles of metal for earrings or cuff links.

AN OVAL PENDANT OR BROOCH

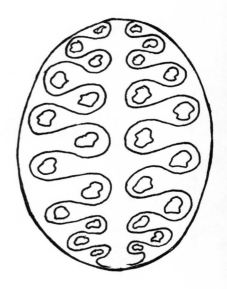

This project is made from an oval copper shape, 2⅛ inches long and 1⅝ inches wide. If you want to make a brooch, buy a shape without a hole at one end. If you want to make a pendant, be sure it has a hole. Or you can cement on a loop of wire with epoxy.

Cover one side with light blue opaque enamel with a little green in it, to make a turquoise color. When dry (about eight hours) add your design. Add squiggly lines in transparent green enamel with a toothpick or a squeeze bottle. Then place transparent red dots inside each curve, again using a toothpick, the squeeze bottle, or a fine brush. Or add enamel lumps.

Let everything dry for 24 hours. Turn over, and support the piece on a metal stilt (see page 15). If a pendant, cover the back with the light blue enamel. If a brooch, leave a broad band clear for the pin back, and cover the rest with the enamel.

Let dry for a week. Add either a jump ring for hanging on a chain, or glue on the pin back.

TICK-TACK-TOE SQUARE

Enamel a 1 inch square of copper with a solid color—either opaque or transparent. When the enamel becomes tacky, form the tick-tack-toe pattern with pieces of enamel threads for the X's, and add either enamel lumps or small dots of liquid enamel for the O's. The liquid dots are added *after* the enamel background has hardened. Let dry until hard.

Glue the squares on cuff link backs or earring backs, or several can be hung on a bracelet chain.

A FREE-FORM
NECKLACE

A very modern shape for enameled jewelry is a copper, free-form design 2⅞ x 1 inches. A hole can be drilled at each end, or wire loops cemented on, to hang the shape on a chain as a necklace.

Enamel the metal in white. When dry, add stripes of different widths at each end to look like a boomerang. Or make a design of many colored, vertical stripes along the full length of metal.

Another design has bits of aluminum foil floating like confetti between two layers of transparent enamel (see page 86 for directions).

Or add enamel lumps or dots of liquid enamel to look like jewels on top of an enameled base.

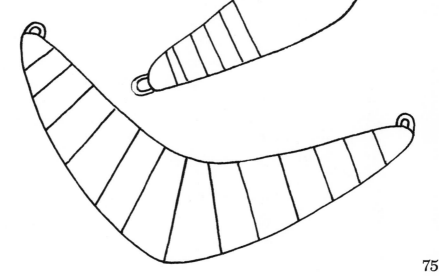

7
BOWLS ❧ AND TRAYS AND OTHER FORMS

Decorating copper or other metal bowls and shallow trays can result in spectacular designs. The basic shapes are bought at hobby or craft shops, or through mail order catalogs. There are many shapes to choose from; oval or round, square or triangular, deep or shallow. Then there are low candle holders, and round covered boxes.

Except for the very shallow trays and bowls, this is a more difficult technique for applying liquid, cold enamel. The enamel will run down the sides, and collect in a pool at the bottom of most bowls and trays. Some of the liquid may stick to the inside, but the surface will not be even. Boss Gloss is the only one of the enamel products with a separate thickener which, when mixed with the liquid, keeps the enamel from flowing down the sides of a bowl.

But here is a trick to overcome the drip! Plan a design, even if it is all in one color, so that you enamel a small section at a time. Turn the bowl or tray on its side, and brace it firmly on a three-prong metal stilt, crumpled newspaper, or a styrofoam block so that it will dry in this position. Now enamel *only* the area that is more or less flat—from the center to the outside edge.

As each section dries, turn the bowl to the next area, and

Triangular, round, and teardrop shaped bowls of gold colored metal, and copper.

enamel. You can separate each section by a band of exposed metal as part of your pattern. After the sections are dry, cover the exposed metal with clear transparent enamel or a contrasting color, to prevent the metal from tarnishing. This whole process will take time, but it is worth it.

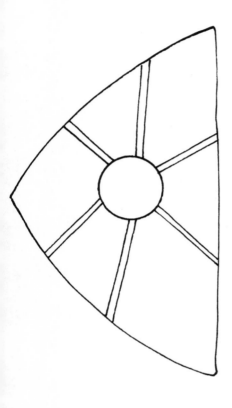

TRIANGLE BOWL

Bowls in several triangular shapes are available in craft shops and by mail order. Some are made of copper, others of aluminum, others of a "base" metal in a gold color. All can be covered with a liquid enamel. Be sure to follow the suggestions on the first page of this chapter for the enameling technique.

The area of the triangle breaks up naturally into smaller triangles and diamond shapes which are separated by strips of the background metal. You can enamel in one color, either opaque or transparent. Or alternate two colors, for instance orange and yellow, and fill the center circle with a third color. Lay out your design on a piece of paper so that the measurements will be even. Transfer the design using carbon paper, scribe into the metal, and clean off carbon.

If you are using a copper triangle bowl, it is best to cover the dividing strips with colorless enamel, as the copper will tarnish and be hard to clean. Or you can use a color to match the color of the center circle. Aluminum or a non-tarnishing base metal can be left uncovered.

A FISH IN A NET

This is a good design for a shallow decorative plate or bowl.

Cover the metal with one or two coats of transparent green enamel. When the second coat has begun to harden, but is still soft, add enamel threads around the edge in a criss-cross pattern. Dry well.

Now add a red or yellow opaque enamel fish in the center. To avoid touching the net area, rest your hand on a wooden block placed on your working surface at the outer edge of the metal form.

Once the front is very hard and dry, cover the back (if it is copper) with either clear enamel or transparent green enamel.

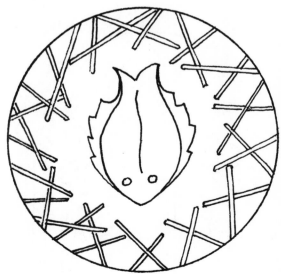

A KALEIDOSCOPE BOWL

Designs for very shallow bowls, or for plate forms are interchangeable. Here are two which can be enameled in a variety of color combinations. Look into a kaleidoscope for other suggestions.

Make a paper pattern to the exact size of your shallow bowl. Follow the scribed lines of your design outline on the polished and cleaned metal. The outline of each diamond is dark blue. The next band is light blue, and the center is a bright green. If you have a steady hand, you do not have to wait for each color to dry. Leave a line of metal between each one. The narrow, angled lines are in dark blue. On a deep bowl, finish each triangle before going on to the next.

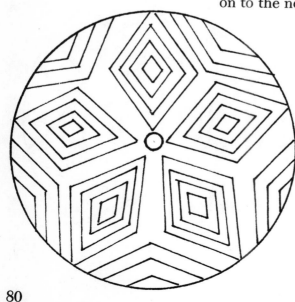

Another design for a flat plate starts with a six pointed star made by overlapping two triangles. A circle is drawn inside the star, touching the bottom between each point. Another star is drawn inside the circle, then a circle, then a star, until the space is filled. Suggested colors; edge green, triangles red, star points yellow; second background triangles pink, star points purple; third triangles green, star points orange; and the last circle in the center is yellow.

A SQUARE TRAY

There are several sizes of copper or other metal trays five or six inches square, with slightly sloping sides ending in a circular center. The outside corners are either square or rounded.

Again make a paper pattern of your design to the exact size of your tray. Transfer it with carbon paper, scribe lines into the metal, and clean off the carbon. Here are two suggestions for projects.

Wide corner areas are enameled in bright blue in the shape of a blunted triangle. Three wide, wiggly stripes in orange fill in the middle of the side areas. If the metal base is copper, cover the in-between areas with colorless enamel

to prevent tarnish. The round center is a bright yellow, suggesting a blazing sun against a blue sky.

For the second design, first cover the copper with either a colorless enamel, or opaque white. The stylized rose and leaves in opaque enamel look just as well on copper as on aluminum, or on a base metal. Fill the center circle with the flower design in red. Yellow dots cluster in the center, and green leaves are placed in each corner.

AN EASTER EGG TRAY

The base of this oval tray can be copper, aluminum, or stainless steel. Usually the shallow tray is about seven inches long, and five inches wide.

This decoration is for fun.

If copper is the base, then the tray should first be covered with a clear, colorless enamel, to prevent tarnishing. When dry, fill in the oval center with an Easter egg design. The one shown here uses pale opaque yellow for the egg shape. Curved bands of orange, both plain and decorative, are outlined with purple. The curved lines make the egg look round. A purple petal design at the small end of the egg has an orange center. Experiment with other color combinations.

The rest of the oval tray is striped in a ray design. Uneven strokes of green enamel are used to suggest a nest of grass.

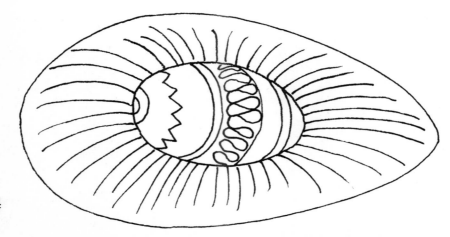

ROUND BOX AND COVER

This formalized flower design is used on the cover of a copper powder box.

Cover the metal top with opaque white enamel. Let it dry overnight until hard, then add the design.

Five long ovals in a flower pattern are centered around a small circle. They are banded with three colors of enamel. Green on the outside, then pink, then a purple center. Between each petal are small circles of pink and purple.

Turn the box on its side and enamel the background area all around with white. Then repeat the small round design of pink and purple on the sides, being careful not to let the colors run down.

If the box is made of spun aluminum, you may want to leave the metal uncovered, except for the design. You may also want to use your own color combinations.

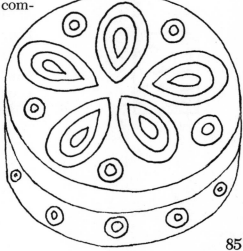

85

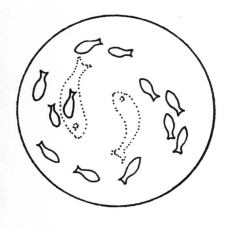

FLOATING FISHES

This shallow copper bowl or plate design includes a new technique of enameling. It is a classic process using *paillons* which means "a large spangle" in French. It is an old effect which used small pieces of silver or gold foil suspended between two layers of transparent enamel. With the cold, air-dried enamels we can use aluminum foil.

Cut a piece of foil 1¼ x 3 inches. Fold in half lengthwise. Next, cut and fold a similar piece of regular typewriter paper. Draw the fish pattern, shown in the margin, on the paper. Slip the folded piece of foil inside the paper. Cut out the fishes, then cut them apart at the center fold.

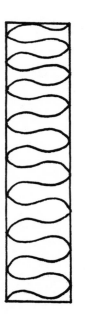

Now, put the first thin coat of transparent light blue enamel on a plate form. Let it harden until it is tacky.

Arrange the fish on the enamel in a pattern. But make a sketch first, so you will know where you want to put them. They may all be swimming together, or separated around the circle. You may want to cut out a large fish or two as a contrast in size.

Let the enamel harden. Then carefully add a second layer over the fish.

They will shimmer under the transparent color.

Here are other variations you might like to try. Add one or two, or more fishes of opaque enamel, in amongst the silver fish before applying the second coat of transparent light blue. You can even add a larger fish in a contrasting transparent color on top of the last coat of light blue enamel.

Or scratch a fish design into the copper with a scriber before putting on the first coat of enamel. Or add one or two white fishes on the metal before adding the transparent blue.

All of these design techniques create a feeling of objects floating in several layers of clear blue water.

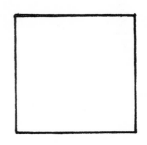

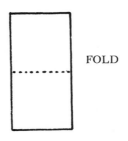

FOLD

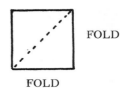

FOLD

FLOATING SNOWFLAKES

Cut out snowflakes from 1⅛ inch squares of foil. See diagrams at right for folding and cutting the designs. Build up layers of enamel and snowflakes, following the directions for floating fish.

FOLD

FOLD

CANDLE HOLDER

A small copper candle holder with a 4 inch base is a good subject for an enameling project. Follow directions for enameling the bowls, using either the sectional method, or adding thickener to the enamel. This is especially important on the upright holder for the candle.

Be sure the enamel is hard and dry before using the holder.

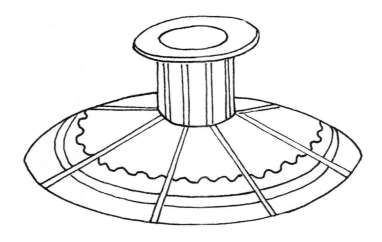

8
SPECIAL TIPS

Spectrum 100 enamel dries hard in twenty-four hours. The lighter colors need three to four layers to bring out the tones. You will need a special liquid cleaner for brushes and measuring spoons. There is no odor to the material.

Boss Gloss enamels are brilliant, deep colors, needing only one or two coats. Color consistency is thick, and some colors solidify in the jars. The powdered thickener works very well with the thinner colors, and does not cloud the transparent enamels. Some of the colors are still tacky after thirty-six hours. Brushes and measuring spoons can be washed off with soap and water. There is no odor to the material.

Ceramitation colors are brilliant, but the material is a bit thin. Enamel stays tacky for more than 24 hours. One drawback is the odor, which is that of an acetate or nail polish, and there should not be an open flame in the room where you are working. A special cleaner is needed for brushes and measuring spoons.

Some of the bright reds of the last two products mentioned dry slowly and remain tacky far too long. This may be due to grease on the metal, a chemical reaction to some metals, or just a fine balance in the proportion of the color and hardener. All enamels should first be tested on a piece of scrap metal before being applied to your design. A non-drying problem *can* be corrected by covering the tacky enamel with two coats of clear nail polish (with drying time in-between applications).

TRANSFERRING DESIGNS

Take a sheet of onionskin or tracing paper, a little larger than the page of this book. Along each edge make pencil marks ⅛ inch apart. Connect the marks with ruled pencil lines until the paper is covered with ⅛ inch squares.

To enlarge any design in this book, cover a sheet of type-

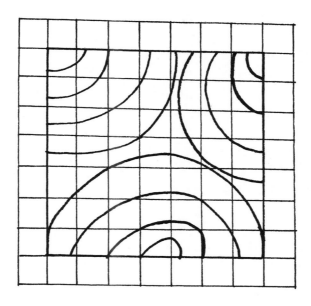

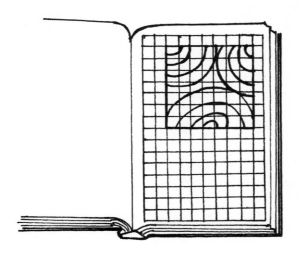

writer paper with large squares, depending on how much bigger you want the design to be. For a smaller design, make the squares smaller.

Now place the onionskin or tracing paper over a design in the book. With a pencil draw the design over the larger squares on the second sheet of paper, copying the lines as they cross the open squares, or follow the vertical or horizontal lines of the smaller squares. In this way you will have a true copy in the right size for your project.

ALPHABET

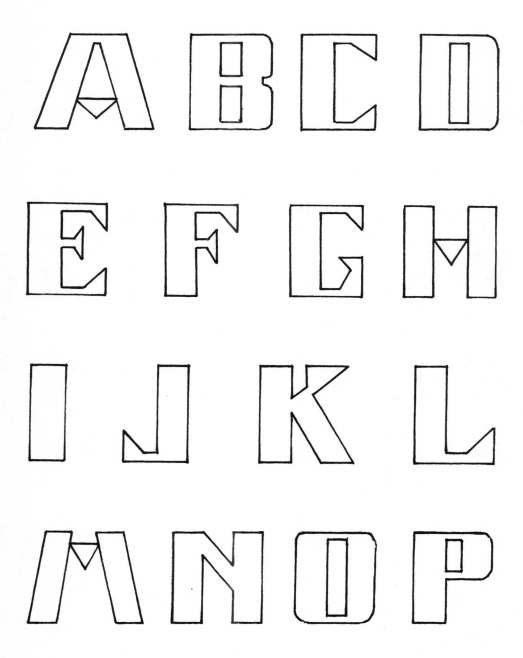

Q R S T
U V W X
Y Z

SOURCES OF SUPPLIES

The following companies will send catalogs, and their supplies can be ordered by mail. For local stores, look in the yellow pages of the telephone book under Artist's Supplies, Craft Supplies, and Hobby and Model Construction Supplies.

Cold Enamel

Abbey Materials Corp.
116 W. 29th St.
New York, N.Y. 10001
Spectrum 100

Romanoff Rubber Co.
153-159 West 27th St.
New York, N.Y. 10001
Ceramitation

Specialty Products
731 Brooks Road
Muskegon, MI. 49442
Boss Gloss

Findings, Metal, and Tools

Allcraft
215 Park Ave.
Hicksville, N.Y. 11801
Retail Store at:
22 W. 48th St.
New York, N.Y. 10036

American Handicrafts Co.
1001 Foch St.
Fort Worth, TX. 76107
(*write for names of local stores*)

American Metalcraft, Inc.
4100 W. Belmont Ave.
Chicago, IL. 60641

Bergan Arts and Crafts
P. O. Box 381
Marblehead, MA. 01945
catalog $1.00

California Craft Supply
Box 3277
Anaheim, CA. 92882

Crown Manufacturing Co.
1188 Industrial Ave.
Escondido, CA. 92025

Davis Crafts
86 W. Old Wilson Bridge Rd.
Columbus, OH. 43085

Gemcraft of Wichita
300 N. Main Street
Wichita, KS. 67202

Gems Galore
1328 El Camino Real
Mountain View, CA. 94040

Gilmans
Hellertown, PA. 18055

The Globe
222 Albert St.
East Lansing, MI. 48823

Greiger's
900 S. Arroyo Pkwy.
Pasadena, CA. 91109

B. Jadow and Sons, Inc.
53 W. 23rd St.
New York, N.Y. 10010

Southwest Smelting
and Refining Co.
P. O. Box 2010
1712 Jackson
Dallas, TX. 75221
catalog $1.00

Lapidabrade, Inc.
8 E. Eagle Rd.
Havertown, PA. 19083

Lapidary Center
4114 Judah St.
San Francisco, CA. 94122

Smokey Mountain Rock Shop
San Carlos Blvd.
Ft. Myers, FL. 33902

C. W. Somers and Co.
387 Washington St.
Boston, MA. 02108

Specialty Products
731 Brooks Road
Muskegon, MI. 49442

The Swensons
9641 E. Apache Trail
Mesa, AZ. 85207

Technical Specialties
International, Inc.
487 Elliott Avenue, W.
Seattle, WA. 98119
catalog $1.00

United Abrasive, Inc.
910 Brown St.
Norway, MI. 49870

Uranium Corner, Inc.
2153 Broadway at Champa
Denver, CO. 80201

U. S. Lapidary Supply Co.
1605 W. San Carlos St.
San Jose, CA. 95128

G. Weidinger
4404 Del Prado Pkwy.
(P. O. Box 5)
Cape Coral, FL. 33904

INDEX

boxes, 33-35, 37, 47, 63, 85
bracelets, 40, 51, 56, 57
Butterfly Pin, 69

Candle Holder, 88
Carpet Tack Design, 49
Coasters, 39
Coat Hooks, 42

Decorative Metal Hardware, 43
Doorknobs, 45
Drawer Pulls or Handles, 44

Easter Egg Tray, 84
epoxy cement, 16-17, 30, 33, 34, 35

findings, 29-30
Finger Rings, 41
Fish in a Net, 79
Floating Fishes, 86
Floating Snowflakes, 87
foil, 11, 27, 75, 86-87
Free-Form Necklace, 75
Free-Standing Name Plate, 67

Gallery Wire Bracelet, 40

Hang up the Washers, 52

Kaleidoscope Bowl, 80-81
Key Chain Charms, 46

Light-Switch Cover or Plate, 38
lumps and threads of enamel, 27,
    54, 70, 71, 72, 73, 74, 75, 79
Lumpy Snail Shells, 72

Metal Boxes, 47, 85
Metal Bracelet, 56

metal, types of, 17-18, 36-37, 53-
    54, 76; cleaning, 16, 19-20;
    polishing, 15-16
mirror frames, 35, 63
Mountings, 55

Nameplate, 66
necklaces, 31, 32, 51, 52, 58-59, 75

Oval Pendant or Brooch, 73

Pendant of Sunburst Threads, 70
pendants, 31, 33, 41, 60, 61, 70, 72,
    73
picture tiles, 64, 65, 68
pins or brooches, 30, 69, 72, 73

Recycled Cans, 50
Round Box and Cover, 85

Sculptured Tiles, 64-65
Serving Spoon or Fork Handle, 48
Small Copper Tiles, 62-63
Square Tray, 82-83
Stick Figures, 71
Sun God Pendant, 61

Tab Bracelet or Necklace, 51
Teardrop Pendant, 60
Tick-Tack-Toe square, 70
tiles, square or oblong, 33-35, 53-
    54, 62-63, 64-65, 68, 70
tools, 14-17
transferring designs, 28, 90-91
Triangle Bowl, 78
Tube Necklace, 58-59

Valentine Bracelet, 57